2. Gloria

3. Sanctus

4. Benedictus

Funky ♩ = c.104

5. *Agnus Dei*

Samba Mass

BOB CHILCOTT

1. Kyrie

With a light bossa nova feel ♩ = *c*.108

Printed in Great Britain

OXFORD UNIVERSITY PRESS, MUSIC DEPARTMENT, GREAT CLARENDON STREET, OXFORD OX2 6DP

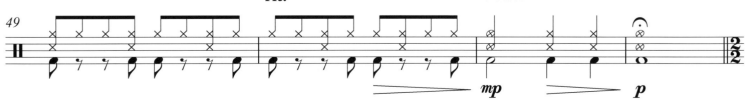

2. Gloria

3. Sanctus

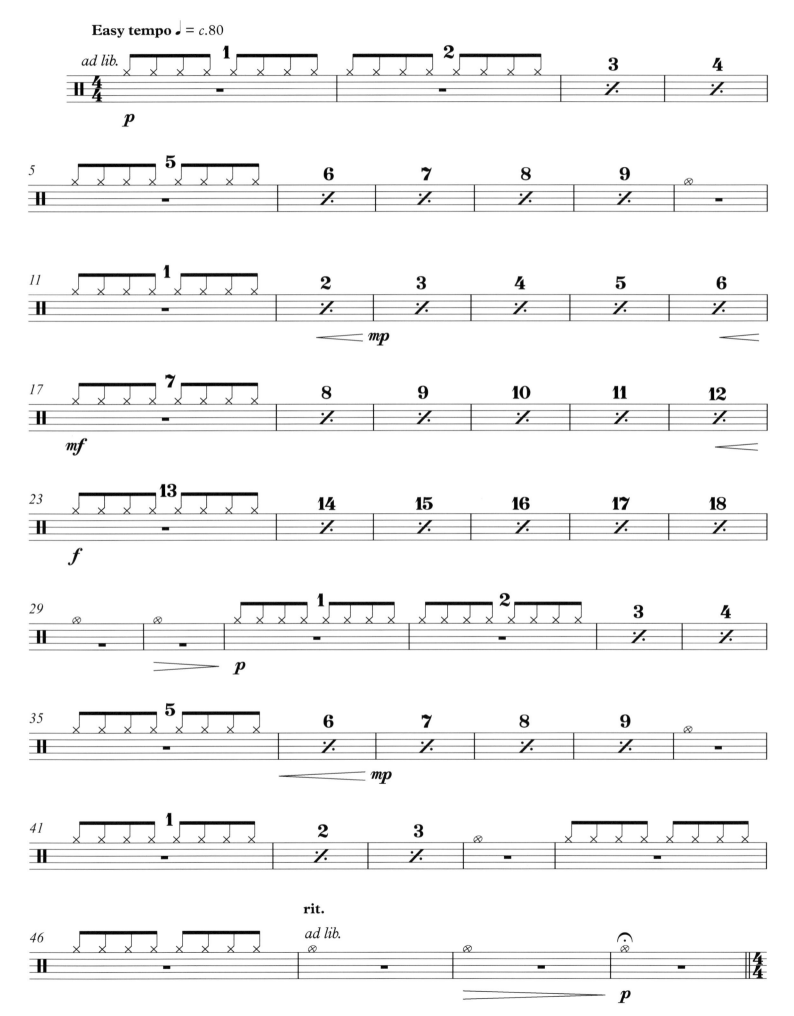

4. Benedictus

5. *Agnus Dei*